Take **5** *for Your* **Dreams**

*five minutes of daily goodness
to make your one-of-a-kind,
never-to-be-on-this-planet-again
life all that it is meant to be* ♥

written by Paula Grieco
in collaboration with Liz McHutcheon

ISBN 978-1-482-34010-5

The main chapters of this book are typeset in Adobe Jenson and Source Sans Pro.
Other typefaces used include: Angelina, Complete in Him, Eurofurence Light,
and Sketch Rockwell.

Photography and other credits: Luis Argerich (Creative Commons), pg. 79; Joshua Barnett (Creative Commons), pg. 84; Creative Commons, pgs. 36, 89, 134; Teresa Ferraiolo, pgs. 102, 106, 109–110, 116; Michelle Gayowski, pgs. 8, 29 (and certain design elements); Garry Knight (Creative Commons), pg. 10; Andre P. Meyer-Vitali (Creative Commons), pg. 16; and Phillip Taylor (ptmoney.com), pg. 119.

Special thanks to the Creative Commons photographers and Teresa Ferraiolo.

Pattern design provided by pattern8.com

Copy editing: Dani Forshay
Creative direction and concepts by: Paula Grieco and Liz McHutcheon
Layout and implementation: Misty Horten

Important Disclaimers

This book is not meant to replace professional support or guidance for you or any other individual. We are not licensed health professionals. If you have any concerns whatsoever about your welfare and safety or that of anyone around you, please seek medical or other professional help immediately.

All the stories and anecdotes in this guide are based on actual interviews and observations. Some names and circumstances have been changed to protect individual privacy while keeping the integrity of the meaning intact.

Dedication

To the one-of-a-kind dreamers in our lives:
Haley and Joshua
Emma and Anna

Authors

Paula Grieco is is a writer, entrepreneur, and amateur photographer. The idea that everyone deserves an opportunity to create an extraordinary and meaningful life runs deep in her personal and professional experience. She lives in Massachusetts with her husband, two children, and dog Henry.

Liz McHutcheon is a recovering CPA, self-taught artist, and small business coach. Liz lives in Massachusetts with her husband, two daughters, and cats Fluffy, Bailey, and Paris.

Join us!

What's Your Brave *is a writing and media project for parents and teen girls committed to giving young women the knowledge and resources they need to live their one beautiful life bravely. To find out more, go to:* www.whatsyourbrave.com.

www.take5foryourdreams.com

Table of Contents

good
courageous
smart lovely
authentic
strong
kind
happy
amazing phenomenal
productive smart lovely
authentic
inspiring
strong
kind good
brilliant happy
amazing phenomenal lovely
productive smart unique
authentic incredible
inspiring
good

INTRODUCTION

"Tell me, what is it you plan to do with
your one wild and precious life?"[1]

—Mary Oliver

Introduction

This is the most important book you will read this year. Don't tell your Calculus teacher, law professor, or boss we said that, but it's true. Too many adults, sadly probably most, don't ever take the time—even just five minutes a day—to think about their lives, their dreams, and what matters to them deep down. Rather than consciously creating a meaningful and happy life, life just happens to them, until one day they look back at all the years that have gone by and feel like they have been living someone else's life, not really their own.

The process of dreaming big and taking practical action to live a life that matters to you starts today.

Being who you really are, living your never-to-be-on-this-planet-again life, can't wait until next year or after high school or college or once you get settled in your career. That's how lives pass, wholly unexamined.

Here are the facts. You are one of a kind. No one like you, not one other person, will ever live on this planet again. WOW! That makes you naturally spectacular! And there is a simple formula to taking your innately spectacular self and creating a life of happiness and extraordinary meaning. So how about it? Can you commit just 5 minutes of your day to a life that truly reflects who you are? That one simple, brave step is how you begin making your life all that it is meant to be.

Once you get started, you'll never want to turn back. It is fun, real, and the only way to live your one wildly precious life. . . After all, the world needs you! If you don't do you, who will?

We are absolutely giddy that you are embarking on this adventure. If you are giddy too, awesome. If not, don't fret. You don't have to feel a particular way to begin living your one unique, beautiful life. You've got this!

How Daily Goodness Works

"Guilt-free" is the most important rule of engagement for this book. We do not want to add to your endless and sometimes overwhelming academic, work, and personal to-do lists.

The process is simple and we will walk you through it every step of the way.

Here's how it works. This book is chock-full of 96 days' worth of daily goodness, including mini-essays, inspirational quotes, and fantastic photos. Your commitment is straightforward. Read one page a day and look for this pink box to find your Take 5 action for the day:

TAKE 5

That means committing just five minutes (which calculates out to .00347 percent of 24 hours, in case you were wondering) a day to reflect on your one-of-a-kind, never-to-be-on-this-planet-again life.

No worries if you miss a day. It's easy enough to pick up where you left off. You are meant to enter a stress-free zone every time you Take 5, so the pace of this book is designed to allow you to take your time! Ready to get started?

P.S. And just so you know, we plan to speak with you like the savvy, smart young woman that you are. As part of the research for this project, we've read an overload of outdated, patronizing books targeted at teen girls and young women. We have learned far too much from loads of amazing girls over the last two years to talk down to you.

A PLACE FOR
DAILY GOODNESS

"Slow down and everything you are chasing
will come around and catch you."[2]

—John DePaola

DAY
01

Are You Ready?

Breathe!

Really, even if it feels awkward. . .just take a moment to close your eyes and breathe in slowly through your nose, gradually filling up your belly with air. And out through your mouth. Five times. Or even two or three times. Don't worry. You have time. We'll wait.

> "Breathe.
> If you feel overwhelmed, breathe. It will calm you and release the tensions."[3]
>
> —Leo Babauta

OK. . .first things first. There is a secret that real-life superheroes have discovered that you are about to find out. And it is so very simple: There is something magical about taking time out of your daily schedule to breathe.

There is something, oooh so spectacular, about creating space internally and externally to consider who you really and truly are, what you love like crazy, and what matters to you deep down. It's where big dreams start, answers come, plans are conjured up, and Divine ideas unfold.

Are you ready to be astonished by earthly miracles?

Setting aside just a few minutes every day with a specific focus will help you rise above the busyness and emotions of daily life to get connected to yourself, and that can change your future!

So over the next few days, you will be creating an awe-inspiring space for your Take 5 (5 minutes, that is) of daily goodness.

For today, if you are feeling stressed or afraid or angry or like you have just way too much to do, try this:

> *Stop. Close your eyes. Breathe in and out slowly, deliberately.*
> Repeat 5 times (or even just once).

Finding Your Place

"In my own little corner,

in my own little chair

I can be *whoever*

I want to be."[4]

—Rodger and Hammerstein's
Cinderella

This is the only time in this book that you will find a quote from a character best known for her appearance in a Disney movie, but Cinderella had a point here.

TAKE 5

Think about your daily schedule. Pick the same time and place for your daily Take 5.

It can be a room, a corner, or a step. Even the bathroom floor works. A place where you can take just five minutes out of your day for some star (that would be you) gazing. It's important that you feel comfortable both physically and emotionally. Somewhere you feel safe to be the rock star that you are.

Collecting Your Treasures

"Once *you* make a decision, the universe conspires to make it happen."

—Ralph Waldo Emerson

TAKE 5

Choose whatever kind of paper appeals to you—a journal, notebook, sheet of loose-leaf paper or even a paper bag will do the trick. You'll also need a pen, pencil, markers, or crayons (your writing and drawing instrument of choice).

That's all you need—this book, paper, and a pen. A timer or alarm that can be set for 5 minutes is also helpful if you have one handy.

If you pay attention to surrounding esthetics, consider adding a candle, a special rock, a quote that inspires you, or other symbolic items. Find a bag or box where you can stash all your Take 5 treasures.

And if you enjoy a little decoupage, decorate your box with your favorite inspirational quotes, photos, and doodles.

P.S. No electronics (including cell phones) within earshot (unless needed for a particular exercise) or if you are using a device for your alarm. Just for five minutes. Kk?

Building Muscle Memory for Your Mind and Soul

Have you ever read or heard a story about an extraordinary professional athlete who is always the first one in the gym or on the field practicing her shot, hit, or kick? What that athlete is doing is creating *muscle memory*. *Muscle memory* isn't literally stored in your muscles, of course, but rather in your brain. Whether you are practicing an athletic move, a song on the guitar, or lines in a play, you will continue to improve when you repeat it regularly because you are building up procedural memory. So now, with that procedural memory stored, your brain can quickly instruct your muscles to carry it out.[5] Voila. . .muscle memory.

Think of your Take 5 go-to place as developing muscle memory for your mind and soul. Go to the same place every day, focus for five minutes, and after a while, your soul begins to be ready for its purpose there.

TAKE 5

This is a good time to confirm that you are happy with your Take 5 place and time. Change it if it isn't working for you. Gather any other feel-good items that you may want to set up around you too. And be sure to have paper and a pen.

Write down the time and place for your Take 5 dreaming spot! Literally, write it in your journal or notebook! There is untold power in committing your plans to paper!

Taking Your Dreaming Spot Wherever You Go

During a bat mitzvah service, a rabbi asked the congregation to take a moment and breathe in and out deeply to take in the extraordinary moment of moving from childhood to adulthood in a young person's life. She went on to explain how this action of breathing in and out—ahhhhh—is the best way she knew to allow such an important life event to truly saturate your psyche.[6] This is one easy way to Take 5 throughout your day; it doesn't have to be limited to your dreaming spot.

TAKE 5

Feel the goodness! Everyday moments can be meaningful too. Think about your schedule today (or tomorrow). Is there a time and place during your day that you feel really and truly free to be yourself or one that you are looking forward to? Maybe there is a friend that you are looking forward to seeing, a class or after-school activity that you enjoy, or a pet that you love spending time with. Write it down now. Enjoy the natural magic by taking a moment to breathe it in today.

natural magic

Enjoying the Moment

TAKE 5

Do you have a favorite song that makes you scream with delight? Or photos that bring back delicious memories? Do you like to draw? Solve puzzles? Take 5 to listen to that song, look at some photos, doodle, or anything else. You decide. The only rule is to do something that you enjoy and feels good.

DAY 07

A Place for Daily Goodness Wrap-Up

You are awesome! By now, you have picked your dreaming spot, selected a meeting time for your Take 5 and have all the magic-making tools you need, like paper, a pen, quotes, etc. for your daily practice.

You are beginning to create your soul-full memory.

And remember to breathe—anywhere, anytime—to reduce stress and be in the moment.

Yippee! Now it's time to become an expert at *being who you really are*. After all, it's a lot easier than trying to be someone else!

> If you would like to go a little deeper on the topic of creating space in your physical surroundings, check out bemorewithless.com

TAKE 5

Go back and browse through what you wrote and read from Days 1–6. Write down one thing that you liked or really stuck with you—maybe a quote that resonated with you, an essay that shifted your perspective, or something you realized on your own. Circle what you picked or dog-ear the page so you can easily find it later.

Quick Review for Days 1-7

- Take time to breathe slowly and deliberately during the day, especially if you are feeling stressed or worried.
- Set aside a time and place for daily goodness to create muscle memory for your mind and soul.
- Gather as many tools as you want for your Take 5, but you'll definitely need paper and a pen.
- Tap into the power of writing your plans and commitments down.
- Use conscious breathing during a special or everyday moment as a method to remember how incredible it felt.
- Enjoy a song, photos, or create something new in your journal.

You are awesome! **creating space**
being who you really are
conscious breathing POWER OF WRITING
mind and soul **magic-making tools**
Take 5 place and time *muscle memory*
JOURNAL dreaming spot

TAKE 5 FOR YOUR DREAMS

PART
TWO

WHAT'S YOUR BRAVE?

BEING WHO YOU REALLY ARE

"Know, first, who you are; and
then adorn yourself accordingly."

—Epictetus

Living Like You Are One in a Million Seven Billion

> *"Always be yourself. Unless you can be a unicorn, then be a unicorn."*
>
> —Unknown

The ancient Greeks and Romans believed that each and every person contained within them a unique, divine guide or inner knowing. What's fascinating is that the Roman word for this inner guiding spirit is the Latin word *genius*.[7] Although today we reserve the term *genius* for a select few with a very specific set of creative or intellectual skills, the Romans were clearly onto something in their original definition.

Consider that there are over seven billion people on planet Earth, and yet not one single person is exactly the same!

Wait!

What?

That is a knock-your-socks-off factoid that is without question spot-on accurate. You are really one-of-a-kind. There is not another single soul on this planet that can live out your purpose—only you. That's quite literally true, so it bears repeating—not one single other soul exists that can express you! Live today like you truly believe that, and you'll change the world!

You're a genius!

Who Do You Think You Are?

Within you is a still small voice.

Some people call it intuition or a gut feeling.

Listen to that voice, that tug, and learn to follow it.

The more you take action based on what you know is right for you,

the louder that spectacular internal leaning will get.

Acting on what you know is right for you takes practice. Simply taking time out to breathe when you have to make a choice is a good place to start.

TAKE 5

Google and write down Shel Silverstein's poem, *The Voice* or another quote that reminds you of the importance of being who you really are. If you feel like your true self is lost under the debris of fitting in, take heart; you are closer than you think. If you are a being you master—tremendous—then share this quote with someone you care about.

Uttering Who You Are

The more you take action to express yourself in a positive way and listen to that whispering voice within, the easier it gets. . .and the more you will love being exactly who you are.

TAKE 5

Today's a day for self-expression. Take 5 right now and experiment by writing freely, doodling words that you love, taking photos of something you think is beautiful with your phone, creating mathematical formulas, brainstorming a cool invention, or drawing a fascinating picture that expresses you. No directions required. No right or wrong answers. You don't need to share it with anyone unless you want to.

Stop Changing

Have you ever been a member of the change cult? Its central doctrine is that changing yourself is the key to being happy. If you change *<fill in the blank here>* about yourself by buying x or doing y, then you will be happier, smarter, braver, and all your dreams will come true. It's no surprise if you feel a persistent need to change yourself, given the barrage of media messages that you are likely inundated with daily. Here are just a few examples from a variety of sources including blogs, television, and the web:

> *Change Your Wardrobe. Change How You Communicate. Hungry for Change?*
> *Change Your Attitude. Change your Thoughts. Talk more. Talk less.*
> *And of course, the secret to all happiness—Change Your Body.*

Growth rocks and is important to being fully human and fully alive, but what if you should start by not changing at all? What if reaching the galaxies begins as you discover and embrace who you already are from the inside out? Try a new take on these perceived weaknesses:

- ♥ You love to be the center of attention? Excellent, get up on stage and share yourself with the world!

- ♥ You're impatient? Good, be impatient to make the world a better place.

- ♥ Bossy? Perfect, we need your leadership!

- ♥ Disorganized? Can't wait to see what you create out of chaos.

- ♥ You're too sensitive? Awesome, people need your perspective!

- ♥ Always seeing the problems in a situation? Imagine how your input can make a product, organization, or school better!

TAKE 5

So how about you? Choose one personality attribute of yours that secretly drives you crazy. Write down one way to look at it anew today in the light of what it brings to the world rather than why you need to change it.

DAY

12

Finding Joy in Being You

Part of the girlhood experience (or the human experience, for that matter) can include an intense desire to win the approval of others. Although this is a natural part of growing up, actively pursuing the momentary gratification of being liked or fitting in can have profound consequences, and likely will leave you feeling empty. Besides, it almost never has the desired impact anyway.

> *"Criticism is something you can easily avoid by saying nothing, doing nothing, being nothing."*
>
> —Aristotle

Every time you make small decisions to fit in, whether as a child or as an adult, rather than being authentic about who you are, you are burying a little part of yourself down deep. This is really serious business, this denying of who you are. Make it a habit, and you *risk becoming confused about your authentic self.* Just search online for books on topics like finding your true passion or how to get back to your true self to get a sense of the energy it takes to find pieces that are lost.

Let becoming who you are rather than the approval of others be your driving force. It's a process, but small decision by decision, begin to act with the courage to be you.

You will probably never meet one human being—not one—who regrets making choices that reflect who they really are. Just like denying ourselves can bury who we are, small decisions to be *you* can have a cumulative impact too. The more often you are brave enough to express who you are, the easier it gets.

TAKE 5

It's a good thing to set boundaries and protect yourself, so this isn't about sharing your deepest, darkest secrets with just anyone.

Here is a good place to start, though. Say or do something today that expresses you without regard to its popularity or commonality. It can be as simple as a wardrobe choice or expressing your opinion respectfully, even if not everyone agrees. Record what you did so that you can look back at it later.

Be Brave

"It takes courage to grow up and become **who you really are.**"[8]

—e. e. cummings

Some people are more naturally inclined to care what others think. If you are one of those people, you also likely have a great propensity to be empathetic.

TAKE 5

Be brave today. When you see someone standing out rather than fitting in, be a voice of encouragement and support. Maybe you know someone that participates in an activity that is considered weird. Take a minute to find out why she enjoys it. Support a friend who wants to try something new, but fears it will be perceived negatively. Or simply don't engage in a conversation that makes fun of someone for being who they really are.

DAY 14

Being Who You Really Are Wrap-Up

You are one in ~~a million~~ seven billion! Living like you believe that definitely takes time, so go easy on the pressure, but really do take it to heart. There is a still-small voice within you that will be easier to hear the more you act on being true to yourself.

Even your *weaknesses* can be expressed in a positive way. If you are having a hard time being who you truly are, start by supporting others who are being themselves rather than seeking the approval of others.

TAKE 5

Go back and browse through what you wrote and read from Days 8–13. Write down one thing that you liked or really stuck with you—maybe a quote that resonated with you, an essay that shifted your perspective, or something you realized on your own. Circle or dog-ear what you recorded so that you can easily find it later.

Quick Review for Days 8-14

- ♥ Remember that you are one in over seven billion—a true genius!
- ♥ Seek to act on your quiet voice within rather than seeking the approval of others.
- ♥ Express your true self privately or publicly. The more you do, the easier it gets.
- ♥ Try to see how a perceived negative characteristic about you can be turned into a positive.
- ♥ Be brave and encourage someone who is standing out rather than trying to fit in.

express your true self **positive** genius

Keep Being You

one in over seven billion discover **BRAVE** true genius

standing out inner voice

encouragement choices

TAKE 5 FOR YOUR DREAMS • WHAT'S YOUR BRAVE?

PART
THREE

WHAT'S LOVE GOT
TO DO WITH IT?

"Do what you love. Know your own bone;
gnaw at it, bury it, unearth it, and gnaw it still."

—Henry David Thoreau

It's (Not) Complicated

Some things in life can be complicated—like Pythagorean theory for musical composition, the quantum entanglement theory, or your relationship with your parents.

Taking steps to live the life of your dreams, however, is not complex, despite what you may have heard on the street. Don't worry if you had this misconception, because there are a ton of people that have some pretty outlandish ideas when it comes to how they should spend their 1,200 months. (If you live to be 100 years old, that's how many total months you have in your one-of-a-kind life.)

Nowhere are these convoluted ideas more evident than in the ways that many people earn a living. Did you know, for example, that many college students major in subjects that they are not interested in, simply because it is "practical" and they think it will help them get a job? No surprise, then, that up to 90% of people dislike their work.[9] Doing dissatisfying work for an average of 2,000+ hours a year is not an option that anyone should proactively pursue.

What's the alternative, then? Becoming a nomad, never committing to anything, living in your parents' basement for eternity, or doing nothing? Definitely not, on all counts!

There is another way. The first concrete step to creating a life—oh so spectacular—is what the next several days of goodness are all about. Become very conscious about what you just plain love to do. Yup—part of making your precious life all that it is meant to be is being clear about when you are fully engaged and what you love like crazy. Simple, right?

> "Often people attempt to live their lives backwards: they try to have more things, or more money, in order to do more of what they want so that they will be happier. The way it actually works is the reverse. You must first be who you really are, then, do what you need to do, in order to have what you want."[10]
>
> —Margaret Young

What Do You Love Like Crazy?

"Don't ask what the world needs. Rather ask—what makes you come alive?

Then go and do it!

Because what the world needs is people who have come alive."[11]

—Howard Thurman

TAKE 5

So how about you? What activities and people make you come alive? Becoming conscious about what you love is a process; enjoy the investigation! You are beginning today. Commit to it right now.

Write down a list of what makes you come alive in your daily life. Anything goes. Consider courses or a particular project in your academic life. How about volunteer work or activities that you really enjoy? Sports, social activities, arts. A job. Maybe it's something that you are really good at, or something you haven't done much of—like traveling—but can't wait to discover what it's like.

If you can only think about the next episode of your favorite reality series, it's okay! Write down what you love about that program.

Start Where You Began

"Fill your paper
with the breathings
of your
heart."

—William Wordsworth

TAKE 5

One of the best places to search for clues to your passions is where you began—
your childhood, that is.[12] Write down what you loved to do in your early years.
Where did you like to be most—at home, outside, at school, or somewhere
else? Did you like puzzles, making books, talking? Maybe movement, drawing,
performing, music. . .?

If you liked this exercise and have time today, ask your mom, dad, or another
trusted adult what you were like as a kid and what you loved like crazy!

Express Your Love Today!

Emma, a high school student, was standing at a white-board laughing with a group of eight-year-olds around her. She was showing them a mathematical puzzle. She promised that no matter what numbers the children gave her, she would come up with the same solution. They were all fully engrossed, laughing, adding fractions, decimals and negative numbers to the formula to try to prove her wrong. But still, she always arrived at the same answer. Magic! The real magic was watching Emma fully engaged in what she loved.

"Let the beauty of what you love be what you do."

—Rumi

Sometimes the way you discover a passion is to try something new—more than once! When you are beginning something whether it be a sport, creative interest, or intellectual pursuit, you may feel more frustration than passion. Stay with it until you develop some level of competency—that's when passion may ignite.

You'll find an example of this tomorrow!

TAKE 5

Express your beauty today! Look through your lists from Days 16 and 17. Pick one thing that stands out as something you love to do. Got it? OK, write it down in your journal. If it is something you can do right now, like drawing or writing prose, do it. Right now! If not, schedule a time on your calendar this week when you will spend just five minutes to express your beauty by doing it.

Exploring New Passions

Sometimes you have to try something new or work through the initial discomfort of the unfamiliar before passion fully kicks in. For Pooja, a high school junior on the West Coast, discovering a new passion started when she accepted an invitation from two friends to join them on a bike ride through the mountains. Pooja remembers how she felt during that challenging day, riding an unfamiliar bike on intense terrain so drastically different from her leisurely spins around neighborhood streets. "I didn't really know what I was doing, [yet at the same time] the adrenaline and control over the bike were *amazing!*

For more about Pooja, go to:

http://whatsyourbrave.com/blog/feeling-the-fear-finding-her-passion/

TAKE 5

Is there an activity that you have observed from afar and would secretly like to try but are afraid to attempt or just haven't had the time for it? Write down what it is and what about it intrigues you.

Discover the POSSIBILITIES

Feel the Love

When you engage in an activity that makes you come alive, the feeling of satisfaction can stay with you long after the moment has passed.

TAKE 5

Think about a moment when you were fully engaged in an activity, task, or event. Look through the previous entries for this section if you get stuck.

Now write down as many details as you can remember about the moment. Where were you? What about it was so special? How did you feel? What in your life today engages you in that same way?

What's Love Got to Do with It? Wrap-Up

Although it seems complicated sometimes, living your dreams doesn't have to be. The first step is to become conscious of what makes you feel fully alive. This is a process; enjoy the investigation, but commit to it today, as it will be one of the most important decisions you will ever make.

Search for clues to your passions by thinking about what you loved like crazy when you were a little kid. Participating in activities that you love feels spectacular deep down, and it's essential to have some time to express that in your current life. Sometimes you have to try something new or work through the initial discomfort of the unfamiliar before passion fully kicks in. Savor the lingering feeling that comes when you are fully engrossed in the moment.

TAKE 5

Go back through Days 15–20 and write down one quote, story, or photo that you loved like crazy! Circle it, mark it with a sticky note, or dog-ear the page so you can remember it later.

Do what you love!

Quick Review for Days 15–21

- Living your dreams doesn't have to be complicated.
- Investigating and becoming conscious of what you love like crazy is a good place to start.
- Thinking back to what you really, truly enjoyed as a child can provide clues to your passions.
- Express your beauty by doing what you love.
- Trying something new can open the door to an unknown passion.
- Savor the feeling of doing what you love.

feeling of satisfaction ENGAGE

living your dreams

DO WHAT YOU LOVE LIKE CRAZY

do what you love SPECTACULAR

try something new ***DISCOVER***

PASSIONS

investigate

WISHES

I wish for a meaningful life.

PART
FOUR

TAKE 5 FOR YOUR DREAMS
WHAT'S YOUR BRAVE?

DEEP-DOWN MATTERS

"I have an irrepressible desire to live till I can be assured that the world is a little better for my having lived in it."

—Abraham Lincoln

DAY
22

The Fast Track Formula to Creating Meaning in Your Life

You matter. Your life matters. Seriously. Your existence makes you innately special. Really breathe that in for a moment. This isn't over-the-top saccharine hogwash; it's an unequivocal truth that too often gets buried in the busyness of everyday activities.

So how does your innately spectacular self create a meaningful life? This is certainly a heady topic and one that philosophers and religious people have pondered since the beginning of human existence.

> "I believe that most of us want to work hard, but we want to do the kind of work that energizes us and makes a positive impact on others."[13]
>
> —Chris Guillebeau

Although there are differences in theories, meaningfulness—that sense that life has importance and purpose—has been consistently linked to "doing things that express and reflect the self, and in particular doing positive things for others."[14] To break it down into a simple formula:

Do what you love + Make a difference in the world = Meaning and purpose

Deb Sterling grew what she loved by getting an engineering degree from Stanford University. While studying, she was troubled that there were so few other young women in the program with her and felt called to change that. She came up with an idea, did a ton of research, invested her own funds, and raised money using crowd fundraising[15] to create a toy company that teaches young girls engineering concepts through books and fun, inventive, and challenging toys—Goldie Blox™. For Deb Sterling's Kickstarter video[16] and more examples, go to the *Resources* section in the back of this book.

This same concept can also be integrated in your daily life starting right now! Think of one activity you are passionate about (or just enjoy) and how you may be able to have a positive impact on someone else's life by sharing it. If you love to draw, spend an afternoon drawing with at-risk kids. Like to talk? Strike up a conversation with someone who seems lonely. The opportunities are endless. Try it just once. It will change your life.

Inventory of What Really Matters

> The secrets out. Devote time to something
>
> *bigger than you*, a something that you really
>
> believe in, and you will *transform your life*.

It's important to be clear about what your values are and what a positive contribution to the world means to you personally—what deep-down matters.

Here's one big hint to get started: Take fame, prestige, and impressing others off the table. Those pursuits may be by-products of going after what really matters to you, but in and of themselves they provide only temporary adrenal rushes with no long-lasting intrinsic value.

Some examples of values (in no particular order) are: your relationship with your family, caring for the environment, helping mistreated animals, discovering cures for disease, caring for the elderly, exploring unknown frontiers, creating art that makes the world a more beautiful place, living your faith, the treatment of women and girls world-wide, education, inventing new technology, living a healthy and active lifestyle. . .

TAKE 5

Write down 3 or more values that matter to you deep down. Another way to think about this question is:

If money, failure, or impressing others were no object, how would you make a contribution to the world? Don't be afraid to go big if that's what comes to mind.

Ask yourself this question once or twice a year.

DAY 24

A Daily Dose of Kindness

"Be *kind*, for everyone you meet is fighting a hard battle."

—Plato

TAKE 5

Big dreams can take time, but you can create meaning in your life anytime by simply taking a few minutes to reach out to someone. Today, while you are going about your usual routine, make a conscious effort to be kind to someone else.

Let a stranger go before you in line for a smoothie, be empathetic to a grouchy waiter, or simply be liberal with your smile. If you are in a situation where you feel uncomfortable, look for a person that seems lost in the crowd or just doesn't seem to fit in, and reach out to her. These little moments, performed regularly, are guaranteed to enhance your life! Don't forget to come back and write down what you did!

Do the Right Thing

"How wonderful it is that nobody need wait a single moment before starting to improve the world."[17]

—Anne Frank

Girls and young women regularly share what courage means to them for the *What's Your Brave?* project[18]. When they give examples of how they have been courageous, it's often not their big adventures or accomplishments. Rather, they recount times when they decided to do the right thing, even when it was extremely difficult—like the time in high school when they chose to stick up for a friend (or stranger) rather than joining in the teasing.

Go to itonlytakesagirl.org to see a short video on how one high school senior, Gabriella Runnels, made a difference. Are you that girl?

TAKE 5

So how about you? What's Your Brave? Every day you have choices to make about doing the right thing. We are all human and so will make mistakes pretty much daily, but was there a time this week when you stuck up for the underdog or expressed an unpopular opinion?

Peas and Perspective

Did you ever hear someone say to a child, "eat your veggies, because there are people starving all over the world?" Although eating food yourself won't do anything to end world hunger, remembering that there are people all over the world who don't have a safe place to live or aren't free to make choices can provide a helpful dose of perspective, especially when everyday circumstances seem insurmountable.

> "The question is not what you look at, but what you see."
>
> —Henry David Thoreau

Isabelle was experiencing some recent shifts in her social relationships and was trying to find her way through them. When an opportunity to participate in a week-long mission trip with her church came up, she decided to give it a try. The trip was her first window into what life is like for children living in abject poverty and very difficult circumstances.

Did her experience make the challenges in her own life go away? No, of course not! But when she saw firsthand the courage of the young children she met, it did give her a pretty big dose of perspective. When Isabelle returned from the mission trip, dealing with her personal difficulties no longer felt insurmountable.

TAKE 5

Ready for a little perspective? Though highly recommended, it doesn't take a mission trip to gain perspective. Pick one world or local issue that concerns you. Even if you can think of ten, pick one (out of a hat if necessary). Read one blog, article, or quote about your issue.

Get Real with Conversations

Connecting with others—soul to soul—creates meaning in our lives.

TAKE 5

Next time you are with friends or adults that you trust, steer the conversation past the empty chatter. Open up a little. Bring up a world or local challenge that you care about, or talk about what's really on your mind. Later, jot down some notes about your conversation.

Deep-Down Matters Wrap-Up

You matter a lot—it's just a fact. The world needs your positive influence. Discover the secret to creating meaning in your life by finding ways to do what you love in a way that makes a positive difference in the world. Once you know what deep-down matters to you, let those values become a driving force in choosing your direction. You can start adding a sense of purpose to your life by being kind to others as you go about your daily activities. Although no one's perfect, practice doing the right thing and having real conversations are other ways to create meaning starting today.

zenpencils.net shares stories and quotes through cartoons! Fun and inspiring all rolled into one.

Speaking of pencils. . .read the story of pencilsofpromise.org founder and how a pencil changed the direction of his life.

TAKE 5

Go back through Days 22–27 and write down one quote, story, or photo that was meaningful to you! Circle it or dog-ear the page so it's easy to find later.

Make a Difference

Quick Review for Days 22-28

- ♥ You are innately spectacular.
- ♥ To create meaning in your life, follow a simple formula:
  - ♥ Grow what you love
  - ♥ Add an issue to which you feel called
  - ♥ Multiply by action
- ♥ Take an inventory of what matters to you deep down.
- ♥ Add meaning to your life by practicing small acts of kindness while going about your daily activities.
- ♥ Doing the right thing is brave.
- ♥ Get perspective by learning about an issue that concerns you.
- ♥ Practice having real conversations with people that you trust.

create meaning in your life **BRAVE**
positive influence *VALUES kindness*
grow what you love
connecting with others INVENTORY perspective you matter

SEEING YOUR FUTURE

"Every great dream begins with a dreamer. Always remember,
you have within you the strength, the patience, and the
passion to reach for the stars to change the world."

—Harriet Tubman

Don't Settle for Boxed Cake

Tara, a high school student who participated in the *What's Your Brave*[19] project, loved science like crazy—particularly astronomy. Seriously, you recognize a passion when you see it, right? Whether you share the interest or not, you want some of that. And what this young woman had was an infatuation with everything science. Her energy was palpable, contagious. The problem is that when Tara was asked about what she dreamed for her future, her answer was "maybe I'll be a cook. . .I like to make boxed cake."

Now, that is how a fish ends up climbing a tree. Tara hadn't yet connected her passions to her future aspirations, partly because she had never been exposed to what her options were. As you begin to become conscious about what you love like crazy and what really and truly matters to you, you are ready to dream dreams and conjure visions. Drama aside, it's time to connect your passions to matching goals. Any size will do small, medium or ginormous!

"Everybody is a genius. But if you judge a fish by its ability to climb a tree, it will live its whole life believing that it is stupid."[20]

—Albert Einstein

Come on, brave idealists, ambitious dreamers, and hopeful believers. This is your moment and it is your time to start putting to paper your truest ambitions. Your BIG BEAUTIFUL life is waiting.

Eighteen Wishes

"Dream lofty dreams, and as you dream,

so shall you become.

Your vision is the promise of what you shall one day be;

your ideal

is the prophecy of what you shall at last unveil."

—James Allen

TAKE 5

Have some fun today! If there were no limits and no chance of failure, what wishes would you truly want for your life? Write down the first things that come to mind. Be specific if you can. Nothing is too ridiculous or unrealistic—remember, the sky's the limit!

Don't extinguish your candles before they're lit. In other words, don't judge your answers or overthink it. This is meant to be silly and inspiring at the same time. Mostly, though, the goal is to make you smile or even giggle with glee!

Start brainstorming! Is there one wish you could make come true?

DAY
31

Star Gazing

"Reach high, for stars lie hidden in your soul.
Dream deep, for every dream precedes the goal." [21]

—Pamela Vaull Starr

Music can remind you to dream deep too! Check out Selena Gomez's *Who Says* and dream big all day!

TAKE 5

Spend a few minutes going through your journal notes from the last few sections—*Being Who You Really Are, What's Love Got to Do with It?,* and *Deep-Down Matters.* Is there a dream hidden in your soul? A goal that is really resonating with you? Or an activity you might want to explore? Be sure to write down whatever comes to mind.

Express what's in your soul!

Look at Her!

There is no one on the planet like you! But that doesn't mean there aren't other women whose lives you see and say, "wow." Role models, both those that inspire you close to home and those you admire from afar is a good place to start as you begin connecting your passions to your real life. Research and exploration take time, but will reap untold benefits.

TAKE 5

Do some exploring today. Spend a few minutes on makers.com and watch some videos of powerful women and how they make a big difference in the world. Bring your journal and note which ones you were drawn to and why. Check out the *Resources* section in the back of this book if you need some help getting started.

DAY
33

Don't Be Rational

"Without leaps of imagination, or dreaming, we lose the

excitement of possibilities.

Dreaming, after all, is a form of planning."[22]

—Gloria Steinem

To continue stirring up the possibilities, check out twitter and learn from motivational experts from all over the world.

TAKE 5

There will be lots of time to be practical about your life, but for today's Take 5, get totally lost in the possibilities. Write about what a typical day would be like when you are all grown up if you could wave a magic wand. Choose one to start, but add as many as you like if you don't want to limit your options! That's what dreaming is all about!

Make a Choice

Rachel Carson was a scientist, writer, and activist. Rachel's plan was always to be a writer; she published her first book at age 11. But after taking a biology course in college and discovering the connection between her love of the ocean and science, she shifted direction radically. Bucking the system, Rachel decided to make an unprecedented choice for a woman in the early 1900s and become a scientist.

> "I am not afraid of storms for I am learning how to sail my ship."
>
> —Louisa May Alcott

Rachel is often credited with being the first environmentalist, discussing the dangers of pesticide use on food in her groundbreaking and widely-acclaimed book, *Silent Spring*.[23]

People who have accomplished great things will tell you that at some point, you have to choose a direction. You can do everything you dream, but sometimes not all of it at the same time. Whether Rachel chose to continue her writing pursuits exclusively or shift to science, she may have ended up in the same place. The important thing is that when the time came, she made a choice.

Although her bold choice to change direction was painstaking for her, as her career evolved she was able to integrate all of her passions—the ocean, writing, and science.

TAKE 5

Get into the habit of making choices, including trying new "stuff" in your everyday life—a new food, hanging out with a different friend, or experimenting with a new hobby. You might uncover a new passion!

DAY 35

Seeing Your Future Wrap-Up

Never settle for boxed cake! Live your wildest dreams by beginning to connect your passions to a vision. Have fun with dreaming and write down your secret (or not-so-secret) wishes. Let who you really are, what you love like crazy and what is deep-down meaningful to you be your guides to creating your dreams.

Part of understanding your options is exploring and research. One good place to start your investigation is by learning about the lives of women whom you admire.

Get into the habit of trying new things and making everyday choices in your life. You can do everything you dream, but sometimes not all at the same time.

If you enjoyed *Look at Her*, then continue exploring role models and heroes to open up your world.

An area that you are passionate about can take you in countless directions. Go to the *Resources* section in the back of this book and spend some additional time getting inspired.

TAKE 5

Go back through Days 29–34 and write about one quote, story, or photo that helped you see your future! Circle it or dog-ear the page so it's easy to find later.

Quick Review Days 29–35

- ♥ Never settle for boxed cake! Begin to connect your passions to a vision.
- ♥ There will be plenty of time to be rational, so take time now to have fun considering your wildest dreams.
- ♥ Dreaming about possibilities is part of planning!
- ♥ Explore the lives of amazing women to inspire you to discover what you are drawn to.
- ♥ Get into the habit of making choices.

dream deep HAVE FUN
connecting your passions
star gazing learning

try new things
never settle EXPLORE CHOOSE

PART
SIX

HOW DREAMS COME TRUE

"Women acquire a particular quality by constantly acting a particular way… you become just by performing just actions, temperate by performing temperate actions, brave by performing brave actions."

—Aristotle

DAY 36

No Magic Wand Required

> *"Action expresses priorities."*[24]
>
> —Mahatma Gandhi

The world is full of dreamers and visionaries. Individuals who dream of expressing their beauty in the world. People who have incredible visions deep down in their souls for how they can bring positive change to the planet. Although their dreams and circumstances can vary drastically, the brave ones that turn their imaginings into reality share one common ingredient. They take. . .

ACTION.

Make a Little Room

> "Things which **matter most** must never be at the mercy of things which **matter least.**"
>
> —Johann Wolfgang von Goethe

TAKE 5

Before you can take action on a goal or dream, no matter how big or small, you have to be sure you have room in your life for taking action. If you have time in your life to pursue something new, then that's good news!

If not, begin thinking of your time as the valuable resource that it is. Is there something optional in your current schedule that drains your energy or you just plain don't like to do? Some examples might be watching too much television or an activity that you no longer enjoy.

DAY

38

Be Brave and Do It Anyway

feel the fear and do it anyway

ONE STEP AT A TIME

take action

DIRECTION NOT PERFECTION

get inspired

learn to know

"Nothing in life is to be feared, it is only to be understood. Now is the time to understand more, so that we may fear less."[25]

—Marie Curie

TAKE 5

Fear is part of life. Period. Often when you are attempting something new, acting different than the crowd, or pursuing a dream that means a lot to you, you will feel afraid. Sometimes people are afraid of failure, of looking foolish, disappointing family and friends. . .

Acknowledge your fear, but continue your work anyway. Action is the best antidote for alleviating fear. And that's what being brave is—not being without fear, but continuing in the right action even when fear is present. Take a deep breath and decide right now that you can be brave when it comes to your dreams. Close your eyes and imagine how exhilarated you feel as you take action on your dreams.

Bit by Bit

Whether your dream is to become a best-selling author, get an A+ in organic chemistry, find a cure for breast cancer, learn how to bake, or be able to rock climb, your goal needs to be divided into smaller steps until the first action on your list feels achievable—almost easy.

If you want more guidance to break down your goals bit by bit, check out Marie Forleo, marieforleo.com. She provides tools and videos to help you take steps to reach your goals.

For example, if you are a new runner, running a marathon may seem like an over-whelming goal. You wouldn't start by running 26 miles on your first run, right? Instead, you might begin by researching some online or smart phone application training programs, selecting a marathon in your area that is scheduled far enough in the future to allow you to complete your training program, maybe choosing to run in order to raise money for your favorite charity, and even purchasing a new pair of running shoes to take care of your body.

As a new runner, on your first time out, you would likely be walking with short running intervals (thanks to the guidance of your online training program). Maybe you would register for interim races beginning with a 5k (3.1 mile) fun-run to get a feel for what it's like to participate in a road race. And finally, you may consider joining a running club to get support and learn from other runners.

This same process—breaking your biggest vision into steps—can be applied to whatever goal you have.

TAKE 5

Look back at the sections: *What's Love Got to Do With It?* and *Seeing Your Future.* Choose a small goal, one of the wildest dreams that you recorded, or select something new. Using your journal, record it now (just for fun) and break down your goal bit by bit into attainable steps.

> "Some people *dream of success...*
>
> while others wake up and *work hard at it.*"
>
> —Author Unknown

Achieving that goal begins when you start to take the actions on your list, bit by bit. The smaller the actions, the better. One step easily leads to another and another. Often just getting started is the hardest part. No matter how you are feeling, push yourself to do something for just 5 minutes and the rest will follow. You may find yourself even working for hours!

TAKE 5

On Day 39, you listed tiny action steps towards something you would really like to do. Do it! Take one tiny action step today.

One action at a time.

Action List Litmus Test

Sometimes when working on a bigger goal, some steps may not make you scream with exuberance.

To use the marathon example, maybe research isn't something that you particularly like to do. However, to purchase the right running shoes, you might need to go online to determine your best options. Always keep the ultimate goal in mind and go back to the true litmus test for what dreams you should spend your time on:

- ♥ Is this goal a self-expression of who you are?

- ♥ Is it meaningful to you?

If the answer is a resounding "yes," then keep taking action.

TAKE 5

Remind yourself what the aim is so you can work through actions that don't excite you.

Using a piece of paper from your journal or a sticky note, write down the goal you have been playing with for the last several days again and why you picked it. Place it in a prominent location like the mirror in your room or keep it in your journal and circle it.

How Dreams Come True Wrap-Up

The world is full of people with astonishing goals. Their dreams and circumstances can vary, but the brave ones that turn their imaginings into reality take *ACTION*.

To start taking action on your goal or dream, make a little room in your life and acknowledge any fears, but be brave and continue your work anyway. Dividing your goal into smaller steps will aid you in taking your first action steps towards achieving your goal. Always keep the bigger goal in mind and go back to the true litmus test to designate which dreams you should spend your time on.

TAKE 5

Go back through Days 36–41. Highlight, dog-ear, or circle (whatever works for you) what one point you most want to remember about taking action.

Quick Review for Days 36–42

- ♥ Your dreams come true by taking daily actions.
- ♥ Make a little room by deleting an optional activity.
- ♥ Be brave and do it anyway.
- ♥ Break your goal down bit by bit.
- ♥ Complete one action.
- ♥ Remind yourself of the bigger goal.

complete one action **THE BIGGER GOAL**
take daily actions
make a little room BE BRAVE
break down goals STEP BY STEP
achievements bit by bit GOALS dreams

STEPPING OUT

"Everything is figureoutable."[26]

—Marie Forleo

Life in the Comfort-Free Zone

It's natural to feel uncomfortable or just plain scared when you are pursuing a goal that means a lot to you, particularly when you are moving into unknown territory. There is typically no way to get around that feeling of discomfort, except to walk through it one step at a time.

> *"Teen girls are sometimes encouraged to sit in a corner, to be quiet...But to do something that you believe in, to go beyond your comfort zone...that's brave."*[27]
>
> —Katherine, Age 18

Take Katherine, a high school senior, who was moved to put her brave into action after learning about the plight of girls who were victims of human sex trafficking. Rather than stand on the sidelines, Katherine decided to take bold action by going right to survivors of this horrendous human rights abuse in The Philippines. She had never been outside of the United States, did not speak Tagalog (the official language of the Philippines), and was a self-described shy person.

After much research and planning, Katherine traveled to the Philippines. Upon returning home, Katherine decided to pursue a vocation that will allow her to continue to travel internationally and empower women and girls who are suffering human rights abuses all over the world. She's a freshman at Stanford University currently and continues to challenge herself to step outside of her comfort zone and pursue what's meaningful to her.

These same principals can be applied to your dreams and daily life, too. Whether it's giving a presentation to a group of peers, having a difficult conversation with a friend, or trying a new sport, getting through uneasy feelings is essential to living your big, beautiful life! If you have ever done it, you know first-hand that there is tremendous personal satisfaction each time you walk through the comfort-free zone and come out the other side. And the best part is, the more you practice, the more confidence you will develop in yourself!

So, what do you say? Are you ready to get a little uncomfortable for your dreams?

Delight in a Brave Moment

"Being brave is doing something that originally inspired fear, but you fought against that fear and moved forward, even though it was hard..."[28]

—Teen girl from whatsyourbrave.com project.

If you want to be delighted and stirred by others brave moments too, Julia Bluhm's story is one place to start. As a teenager, she took on *Seventeen* magazine. Read more about Julia at SPARKsummit.com or find her on TEDx.

TAKE 5

Do you remember a time in your life when you stepped outside of your comfort zone? Write it down in your journal. Recall as many details as you can—how did it feel, before, during, and after. How did it change your perspective? Close your eyes and take a moment to congratulate yourself for being brave in that moment!

DAY 45

Explore the Possibilities

fairy dust

"If I had influence with the *good fairy* who is supposed to preside over the christening of all children, I should ask that her gift to each child in the world be a *sense of wonder* so indestructible that it would last throughout life."[29]

—Rachel Carson

TAKE 5

Do you have a sense of wonder? Is there something that is meaningful to you deep down that you want to pursue, even the thought of it makes you feel uncomfortable? Traveling somewhere new, volunteering at a horse farm and helping to deliver colts, interviewing the curator at your favorite art museum are just a few of the endless possibilities. What's yours?

Begin by developing a sense of wonder. You won't make any progress by sitting on the couch and thinking about it forever, so start learning as much as you can about your destination. Explore!

I Don't Know

Sometimes people lose their way toward their dreams or never felt like they had a path in the first place. Did you ever feel like you were unsure about what you want? That, if you were to be completely honest, you really just don't have any idea who you are? Or sometimes people can know exactly what they want but don't believe they can make it happen.

"A person grows most tired while standing still."

—Chinese Proverb

Remember that you are one-of-a-kind already, so take the pressure of having to figure it all out right now off of yourself... Really just let it go. Acknowledging that you don't know your way is the first step in moving forward.

Then it's time to step out of that cozy spot of standing still. Allow yourself the time and space to investigate different options in depth. Take action even if you don't believe in yourself quite yet. Try something new on for size.

Creating the habit of listening and acting on your voice within can help you find your way. Check out Christina Aguilera's song *The Voice Within* and really take in the words.

TAKE 5

Become an investigator by learning about one area that you are interested in (or potentially interested or have a very slight inkling that at some point you may want to pursue further). The first step is to pick something, just select one thing to get started. Don't worry, your commitment is to exploration only! Write it down.

Change Your Mantra

Do you know what Hannah's talking about?

No matter where you would rate yourself on the self-confidence scale, you have likely said mean things in your own head about your abilities or your intelligence or the way you look. This negativity can keep you from moving forward (aka, keep you in a negative comfort zone) and make you feel even more discouraged. There is another choice, though! You can ignore or change that voice and move forward one small step at a time anyway.

> "...Any mean thing someone's gonna think of to say about me, I've already said to me, about me, probably in the last half hour!"
>
> —Hannah Horvath, "Leave Me Alone" Episode of *Girls*

TAKE 5

Create a positive mantra—a statement that is repeated—to shift your focus. Examples of mantras are:

I am moving forward in a positive direction anyway!
I am taking one step at a time toward my dreams!
I accept myself just the way I am.

Pick one of these or make up one of your own and write it down. Next time you find yourself in the middle of an unfriendly conversation with yourself, try this: simply breathe, repeat your mantra, and proceed in a positive direction anyway.

Looking Up

Sometimes we step outside of our comfort zones and it exceeds all our expectation. A new tri-athlete pushes through her discomfort by completing her first open water swim and experiences the exhilaration of finishing her first race. Or a student that fears public speaking, delivers a speech in front of an entire class and feels excited about the prospect of finding more opportunities to speak in public. Other times though, the result isn't what we hoped for. The tri-athlete gets a cramp during her run and needs to stop before she's completed the race.

Either way, you are moving forward on your journey. In both cases you are brave.

"So go ahead. Fall down. The world looks different from the ground."[30]

—Oprah Winfrey

TAKE 5

Everyone experiences defeat or makes mistakes. Can you think of a time when you experienced a setback? How did you (or would you now) get through it to keep moving forward? When stepping out of your comfort zone doesn't prove to be what you were expecting, learn from your view on the ground, adjust your next step as necessary, and just keep moving forward.

Stepping Out Wrap-Up

It's not uncommon to feel uncomfortable or scared when you are trying something new or pursuing a dream that means a lot to you. The only way to get past that feeling is to walk through it even if you don't believe you can. Keep in mind those times that you have stepped into the uncomfortable and made it successfully to the other side.

Sometimes not knowing what to do next can keep you from moving forward. Step out of your comfort zone by developing a sense of wonder and becoming an investigator. Most everyone has times of self-doubt or negativity, but shift your focus by creating a positive mantra and continue to progress. It's okay to fall down and sometimes results aren't what we wanted. Learn from your misstep and adjust as necessary.

TAKE 5

Go back through Days 43–48. Highlight, dog-ear, or circle (whatever works for you) what one point you most want to remember about stepping out of your comfort zone.

You are brave!

Quick Review for Days 43–49

- ❤ It is natural to feel uncomfortable when you are pursuing a goal that is important to you.

- ❤ Remind yourself often of times when you have stepped outside of your comfort zone.

- ❤ It's OK to be unsure how to move forward; try developing your sense of wonder.

- ❤ Become an investigator and learn about something you have even a slight interest in.

- ❤ Create a mantra to help shift your focus to the positive and keep you moving forward.

- ❤ Sometimes results aren't what you expected. Keep moving forward in a positive direction.

learn something new **positive**
sense of wonder
KEEP MOVING FORWARD be brave FOCUS
comfort-free zone **stepping out**
investigate positive mantra

PART EIGHT

YOUR PASSION TRIBE

"We need support. We need a hand to pull us up
off the ground when we get kicked down in the arena
(and if we live a courageous life, that will happen.)"[31]

—Brené Brown

DAY 50

Inside the Circle

Your peeps, your circle of friends, your confidantes, parents, trusted advisors, call them what you want. Whether you are naturally more inclined to enjoy solitude or to be with other people all the time, everyone needs to have an authentic group of friends and advisors.

> *"I felt it shelter to speak to you."*
>
> —Emily Dickinson

Think of it as your passion tribe, those in your life that are there to support you in being all that you are meant to be.

These are the people you can depend on to be there when you need them to encourage you—the ones that celebrate your successes and help you stand back up after you make a mistake. Your passion tribe includes the first people you go to when you have some exciting news to share or have had a really bad day.

Whether you have a tribe now or need to develop one, your inner circle typically includes advisors such as parents, teachers, guidance counselors, or other trusted adults, and a few or more peers whom you can rely on.

Sometimes, finding these go-to peeps can feel overwhelming, especially during high school. But you can do it by thinking about and exploring potential options for connecting with others who share your interests!

Stick with it as you read through the next several days and get the advice you need from a parent or other trusted advisor.

Can You Listen to Me?

"A *friend* is one that knows you as you are, understands where you have been, *accepts* what you have become, and still, gently allows you to *grow*."

—Accredited to William Shakespeare

The research is in. Having adult advisor(s) in your life that you can talk to, whether it be to share exciting news or to talk through challenges, has a positive impact in your life for the long-term.[32]

This isn't about someone handing you a detailed how-to manual with instructions on how to be you. But whether struggling with a social conflict, how to pursue your boldest dreams, or anything in between, a trusted adult and mentor can provide the sounding board and support you need to work through challenges.

TAKE 5

Today, take a moment to think about the adults in your life who have your back. Maybe it's your mom, dad, guardian, aunt, grandparent, or an older sibling. Perhaps a teacher or guidance counselor at school comes to mind as someone you could talk to. Write down who is on your go-to list. Next time you are working through a challenge, don't go it alone. Reach out and ask for a listening ear to provide you the support you need.

DAY 52

Just Plain Fun

"No, I'm not being immature, *I'm having fun* You should try it."

—Author Unknown

TAKE 5

What's just plain and simply fun for you? Do you prefer to hang out with a large group or are you more of a one-on-one type of gal? Make a list of how you like to have wholesome fun. Do you like to watch old movies, take walks in the woods, sing karaoke, bake, draw, talk about politics or religion, work on math puzzles, or listen to music? Maybe it's being able to act weird and still be accepted for who you are.

Keep Good Company

Rachel is a talented and creative student, but her high school social experience is difficult for her. Unwilling to compromise who she is, Rachel dresses in what might be categorized as very alternative clothing, at least in her local community. In contrast, she attends a suburban high school where jeans, trendy boots, and t-shirts are the "uniform" of choice.

Have you listened to any music by singer/songwriter Vicci Martinez? Check out her song *Come Along* and be reminded of the freedom of not going it alone.

When Rachel discovered a paid internship at a local art and media organization in the city, Rachel jumped on the opportunity. There she was able to connect with like-minded adults and peers who supported her in her uniqueness and celebrated her creative pursuits. Although her high school social experience was still challenging, Rachel was able to get through the difficulties and thrive thanks to all the support she received at the arts program.

TAKE 5

One of the best ways to grow your dreams and expand socially is to find a group of supportive peers with whom you share a positive interest (even if you're just curious about exploring it). If you want to get more active, join a running team or triathlon club. If you like to speak in public, how about a debate team? If you enjoy acting, then a theatre group may be for you.

Be sure to suspend your judgments of what is hip and just go for what interests you.

There are countless organizations to choose from like: Science Club for Girls, YWCA, Girls Inc., etc. So how about you? Do you want to further develop your circle of peeps? See the *Resources* in the back of this book if you need help getting started. Spend a few minutes right now and Google local organizations for teens and give it a try!

Don't Go It Alone

Every day Shayna dreads her math class. The problem isn't the subject or her grades, but rather a group of younger boys in her class who skipped ahead a year in math and have begun to mock Shayna. Anticipating relentless commentary from them like, "How could you ask such a stupid question in class?" makes even walking into math class some days an act of everyday courage.

> "There is nothing I would not do for those who are really my friends. I have no notion of loving people by halves, it is not my nature."
>
> —Jane Austen

Rather than tolerating this toxic environment alone, Shayna turned to her teacher, parents, and her friends for support. She talked about the situation a lot with her friends and made sure to meet up with them before and after math class whenever possible.

Getting support is super important. Girls and young women from the What's Your Brave project often share how invaluable organizations like *Girls for a Change* have been in providing a life-changing support system. Check out the *Resources* section for more.

TAKE 5

Whether it's supporting you in times of trouble or encouraging you to pursue a dream, supportive friends and adults will enrich your life and make the going easier through difficult times. Write about a time when you were there for a friend or she was there for you.

Be a Friend

At some schools, colleges, and workplaces, it is a tradition to acknowledge birthdays in a small but special way. Maybe a card, a cupcake with a candle, decorations on a desk, etc. This is really thoughtful and fun, but for some girls it is always a source of worry that no one will remember them in that special way.

TAKE 5

One of the surest ways to increase your inner circle is to be the friend you want to have. Brainstorm a list of ways that you can surprise someone with an act of kindness and friendship on any day of the year.

Is there someone you know that may be off the radar? Make a congrats card for friend who finished a big running meet. Go out of your way to acknowledge and hug a friend who did well on an important test. Or you could do the same if you know someone is feeling down because she was embarrassed in class or didn't get a part in the play.

DAY 56

Passion Tribe Wrap-Up

Creating a passion tribe can feel like a big challenge at times. One place to start is by seeking out mentors and advisors like family members, teachers, and others that you can go to for encouragement and support. This will be invaluable to you as you follow your dreams and get through times of difficulties too. In addition to adults, developing a circle of like-minded peers whom you can count on will contribute to your personal well-being. Consider finding an organization where you can pursue fun activities and interests that you are passionate about. This is just one way to start to grow personally and develop lasting friendships. Be the friend that you want to have by reaching out to those that look like they could use a little encouragement.

Remember to invest in connecting with others who share a similar passion. Check out the *Resources* in the back if you need a place to start.

TAKE 5

Go back through Days 50–55. Highlight, dog-ear, or circle (whatever works for you) what you want to most keep in mind about creating your passion tribe.

You're invaluable!

Quick Review for Days 50–56

- No matter where you fall on the extrovert/introvert spectrum, everyone needs support from others.
- Your circle can include friends, parents, and other relatives, mentors, etc.
- Research shows that having a trusted parent or adult advisor/mentor will have a positive long-term impact on your life.
- Incorporating fun and your passions into your life is one way to expand your friendships.
- Consider joining an organization focused on a passion or a potential interest to develop authentic connections with others.
- Make it a habit to reach out to others when you are going through challenging times to diffuse the difficulties.
- Be the friend you'd like to have.

diffuse the difficulties FOCUS
reach out to others
POSITIVE LONG-TERM IMPACT
circle of friends KINDNESS fun
expand friendships*dreams* SUPPORT passion tribe

THE SECRET TO DEVELOPING YOUR SUPERPOWERS

"The most effective way to do it, is to do it."[33]

—Amelia Earhart

The Hard-Working Superhero

Do you know a superhero? Here are some to get started:

Pink	Martin Luther King, Jr.
Sheryl Sandberg	Sejal Hathi
Oprah Winfrey	Julia Bluhm
Eve Ensler	Debbie Sterling
Kathryn Bigelow	Angela Zhang

> *"We are what we repeatedly do. Excellence then, is not an act, but a habit."*
>
> —Aristotle

These real-life superheroes all make their craft look effortless. But the truth is, the way to make your wildest dreams come true begins with a vision, followed by *repeated daily work*. Sometimes that work can feel easy, but other times, even if you are passionate about an endeavor, discipline and habit are required to make progress.

We often think of Martin Luther King, Jr., one of the greatest orators of all time, as just naturally gifted and inspired. Perhaps, yes. Did you know, though, that hard work and effort, rather than natural abilities, are the truest indicators of success?[34] And even Martin Luther King is no exception. He also worked tirelessly on developing his speaking techniques through formal education, memorization, and exchanges with his peers. During his *I Have a Dream* speech, King spoke extemporaneously while delivering the most powerful sections. But he was ready for this historical moment because of all the time he had spent developing his oration skills and knowledge![35]

And it isn't just him. Although there may be an infrequent exception, most superheroes from all walks of life have a vision but then work hard every single day to do the personal and professional work required to turn their dreams into reality.

Pink is another great example of this. Although her first album was well-received by the public, it didn't reflect who she really was. Instead of settling for the public accolades, she devoted her energy to developing a "deeper, edgier sound." She wanted to work harder to be herself. [36]

When you are doing something that you love in an area that matters to you deep down, then there is untold gratification even when times are tough.

So what do you think? You are the real-life superhero, no cape required. Are you ready to develop your superpowers?

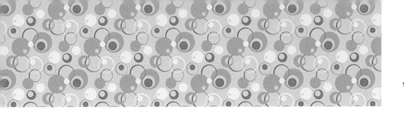

Just Show Up

"My sophomore year of high school, *I decided to try* cross country. I didn't <yet> have the endurance or an athlete mindset. For me, *it took a lot of bravery* to go out that first day and then to keep showing up. As a result, I became a runner."[38]

—Jessi, Age 17

For more on creating healthy habits, check out zenhabits.net.

TAKE 5

Showing up for your dreams is the first step to developing your superpowers. Mollie, above, shows up at the track every day, Aly Raisman shows up at the gym every day, Angela Zhang shows up in the science lab, etc.

Write down where you can show up today.

Creating Habits

DAY
59

Taking It One Step at a Time

Living your dreams can be exciting and energizing, but sometimes it can feel like hard work. Whether your glass is half-full or half-empty is irrelevant; either way, you can do the work one step at a time.

TAKE 5

Just in case you haven't realized it yet, you are developing your hard-working superpowers every time you complete a Take 5. And by the way, your completion of Take 5 tasks do not need to be perfect; that's only for the guys with the capes.

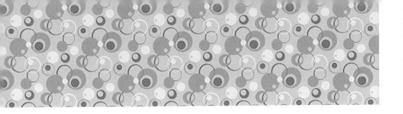

Give Yourself a Break

Feeling continued resistance while doing an activity can mean it is time to be gentle with yourself and give yourself a break.

> Did you know that getting the rest you need will make you more productive?

Here's one concrete example adapted from a habit master, Leo Babauta.[39] This advice was intended for the writing process, but it can be applied to other areas as well, like studying, athletic practice, science and mathematic challenges, etc. When you sit down to write and start to feel resistance to the writing, work through the resistance for two minutes before stopping for a minute. This second time, push through the resistance for a little longer—maybe three minutes before stopping. Then write again. As soon as you feel resistance on this third round, take a five-minute break. Over time, increase the length of time you spend pushing through the resistance. Sometimes walking away from your efforts for a few minutes will be all you need. The key is to be gentle with yourself and expand slowly.

TAKE 5

Are you feeling any resistance today?

Not to worry, just take a break.

Be gentle with yourself.

DAY 61

Learn from a Hard-Working Superhero

Whether it is a hard-working superhero in your own life, someone famous you admire from afar, or one that's on the list earlier in this section, you can learn a lot by just checking out the scoop of someone you admire and how they got where they are. At minimum it will inspire you!

Go to the GoodLifeProject.com for an abundance of video interviews of hard-working and successful real-life superheros.

Tavi Gevinson, a teen girl, had a hard time finding strong female, teenage role models, so she built a social media site where they could find each other. Listen to her TEDx talk, *a teen just trying to figure it out* to hear more.

TAKE 5

Can you think of someone you admire? Write down who it is and why their work inspires you. If you can't think of one, Google one (or as many as you like) from the list on Day 57!

What Are You Up to Today?

Your days, especially if you are in school, can be pretty jam-packed with classes, studying, and extracurricular activities, sometimes passing like one big blur. It's important to periodically take a step back and think about how you are spending your time.

TAKE 5

Take a few minutes to mentally go through your day. Is there an optional task or activity in your schedule that consistently leaves you feeling drained? Can you take that off your schedule today?

DAY 63

The Secret to Developing Your Superpowers Wrap-Up

Although real-life superheroes make their crafts look effortless, it actually takes daily hard work to turn a dream into a reality.

Developing your superpowers (also known as habits) will be easier on some days than others, but keep moving forward, bit by bit, and you will make progress. Be sure to remind yourself that it is okay to take a break. Perfection is not the goal. And above all else, remember that you are amazing!

TAKE 5

Go back and browse through what you wrote and read from Days 57–62. Write down one thing that you liked or really stuck with you—maybe a quote that resonated with you, an essay that shifted your perspective, or something you realized on your own.

Be your own superhero.

Quick Review For Days 57–63

- ♥ Developing your superpowers is hard work.
- ♥ Where can you show up for your dreams?
- ♥ Whether your glass is half-full or half-empty, do the work anyway.
- ♥ Feeling resistance? Take a break.
- ♥ Google a superhero for inspiration.
- ♥ Find five minutes in your day to practice your superpowers.

living your dreams **get rest**
superpowers
REPEATED DAILY WORK DREAMS
superhero *HARD WORK* effort habits
inspiration practice

PART
TEN

TAKE 5 FOR YOUR DREAMS
WHAT'S YOUR BRAVE?

BODY BRAVE

*Body Brave (v): Consciously choosing to
love your body and be you every day*

The Cultural Body Vibe

What does your physical appearance have to do with living your one-of-a-kind life? Nothing really, but you would never know that if you spend any time watching media of any kind.

> "There are many things that are out of your control (like…rainstorms, skinny jeans, and tube tops) yet you actually have a lot of power over your health, happiness, and life. . ."[40]
>
> —Kris Carr

You probably don't need research to know this, but girls are inundated with messages about what they are supposed to look like (and dress like and talk like, etc.) more than a quarter of a million times before they reach adulthood.[41] The American Psychological Association found that the media emphasizes young women's sexuality to *"a stunning degree."*[42]

This toxic script comes from every media imaginable: television, music videos, music lyrics, movies, magazines, sports media, video games, the Internet, social media, advertising, and toys.[43] It also comes from the interpersonal relationships in your everyday life.

If you are female, you have likely experienced firsthand what it is like to be judged first and foremost by how closely you match a beauty standard that is not realistic. Literally, the standard is unattainable[44] because most of what you see has been altered and enhanced using digital tools like Photoshop.

Becoming educated about these issues is critical because research shows conclusively that they can have subtle to profound consequences on your psychological, physical, and emotional well-being.[45] Too much focus on physical appearance takes significant time and energy from what's really important—like discovering your dreams, developing your character, and being the one-of-a-kind, never-to-be-on-this-planet-again person that you are!

Thankfully, the narrative doesn't end there. There is a movement to change this toxic script. If you struggle with body image, you are definitely not alone. The next several days highlight actions you can take to become a more media-savvy consumer and begin to protect yourself from these harmful messages.[46]

Watch What You're Watching

Seijah, a high school student, experienced a pivotal aha moment after reading a book about the definition of beauty in different periods in history,

"I remember reading that at one time it was considered beautiful to be morbidly obese, and I realized that the idea of <external> beauty was more an illusion than a reality...I have a very strong idea of who I am... *when I listen to songs or watch media,* I see that the <expectation> is to have a specific type of body, have a specific type of hair, wear make-up, and it takes *courage every day* for me to not give into that and be who I am."[47]

—Seijah, Age 17

TAKE 5

Think about the last time you watched a television program, attended a sporting event, shopped at a mall, or flipped through a fashion magazine. Consider the messages given to girls and women through those media outlets. What is a typical advertiser trying to sell you by making you feel like you are not good enough the way you are?

If you need some help to get started, check out the body image *Resources* at the end of this book.

Eat Your Veggies

Start to think about your body as the tool you need to accomplish your dreams and goals. In other words, focus more on health than physical appearance.

TAKE 5

Good and nutritious food is what fuels your body and gives you the energy you need to live your big life and bold dreams! Eat an apple today (or another fruit or veggie of your choice). Repeat at every meal. If you are interested in learning more about how to properly fuel your body with food, check out the *Resources* section in the back of this book.

Get Physical

Regular exercise will change your life and even your brain chemistry. It's true. It will make you sharper while doing work and can also help improve your mood. Whether you label yourself "athletic" or not is irrelevant. Focus on being strong and moving your body rather than meeting some bogus and artificial standard. Be strong!

TAKE 5

Put down your pen and move right now. Jump up and down 20 times, do ten jumping jacks, five push-ups, walk or march in place, whatever you like. Just move! Consider continuing this daily as part of your Take 5. Perhaps you can set a goal to improve your personal best. (For example, if you can do just one push up today, then set a goal to work up to ten, bit-by-bit.) Write down what you did today. Record your goal too if you have set one.

You're STRONG!

DAY
68

> "I realized that I don't have to try to look like someone
> else or mold myself into my surroundings...
> I can be and look like who I am
> and still be happy."[48]
>
> —16 year old teen girl

At its best, beauty and style can be fun and a part of your self-expression. Stephen Chobsky, author and director of *The Perks of Being a Wallflower*, commented on his favorite scene in the film: "There's nothing like that first moment when you realize that there are people in this world who will accept you for being exactly who you are." [49]

That is what *Body Brave* is all about—embracing our unique, amazing selves, bodies and all.

TAKE 5

Write down a way you can express yourself today. Maybe through a wardrobe choice, expressing your opinion in class, or another way that is particularly meaningful to you.

Change the Focus

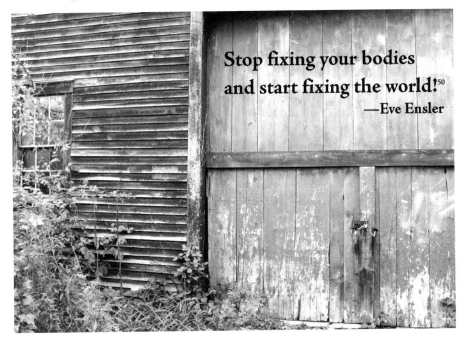

Stop fixing your bodies
and start fixing the world![50]
—Eve Ensler

TAKE 5

Stop trying to fix your body and start taking care of yourself! Be gentle. Create your own personal graffiti wall in a journal. List personality and physical attributes that you admire about yourself. Focus on how you can contribute to the world (more on this later).

Body Brave Wrap-Up

If you are a girl living on the planet Earth, then it is hard to escape the bombardment of messages telling you what you should look like, wear, etc. Although you can't avoid the messages, you can become a critical observer and educate yourself on these negative influences. Becoming aware of this issue and its impact on you is important because too much focus on physical appearance takes significant time and energy from what's really important!

Start to think of your body as a tool by practicing good hygiene and eating lots of fruits and veggies to fuel your body. Regular exercise can change your mood and your life. If you need to make health changes, start slowly and get the support you need.

Be gentle with yourself. Focus on what you like about yourself and how you can develop your skills and make a difference in the world rather than trying to fix your body.

TAKE 5

Go back through Days 64–69 and write down one thing that you liked or really stuck with you. Be sure to circle or dog-ear what you recorded so you can find it later.

♥ The media inundates girls with false messages about their physical appearance and an unattainable standard of beauty.

♥ Arm yourself by becoming a critical observer of the media and what they are really trying to sell you.

♥ Start to think of your body as a tool; practice good hygiene and eat well to energize yourself so that you can focus on what really matters.

♥ Moving your body and exercising can have a multitude of positive benefits.

♥ Think of your physical appearance as another form of self-expression.

♥ Be gentle with yourself and focus on what you like about yourself physically and in terms of personality characteristics.

♥ Check out the *Resources* section at the end of this book for more information on body image. *A reminder that this book is not intended to replace professional medical support and advice.* If you have any concerns, please seek medical or other professional help immediately.

positive benefits **take care of yourself**
self-expression *BODY BRAVE* **SKILLS** exercise PERSONALITY
standard of beauty
be a critical observer CHANGE THE FOCUS

PART
ELEVEN

GROWING YOUR ASSETS

"Far away there in the sunshine are my highest aspirations. . .
I can look up and see their beauty, believe in them,
and try to follow where they lead."

—Louisa May Alcott

Your Priceless Assets

"Invest in yourself. It will pay you for the rest of your life."

—Aristotle

What's the first thing that comes to mind when you hear the word "assets"? If you are like most people, your first word association is "money" or other "material possessions." For good reason. In our society, financial wealth is one of the most common prestige meters. **And to be fair, making a significant income is a really good thing!** Money is certainly a baseline necessity in our culture.

Consider, though, that you own and can invest in other assets that are priceless. These assets are your highest attributes: your character, courage, tenacity, education and intellect, creativity, skills, kindness, strong and active body, time, good work ethic, generosity to others, personal relationships, etc.

As you Take 5 over the next several days, be open to shifting your focus to this broader definition. Just think, by simply completing your daily Take 5, you are already increasing your personal net worth.

This alternative perspective isn't about ignoring your financial health or cavalierly pursuing what you love without having a plan for how you can make money. In fact, when weighing options for your future, financial gain should be on the table as an important consideration.

But investing in you is a sure-fire way to grow assets that will reap dividends, financial and otherwise, for a lifetime. After all, your life and your world are an expression of the investments you've made in yourself.

As part of growing all your assets, go to suzeorman.com
and learn more about your financial health.

Say "Thank You"

"If the only prayer you said was *'thank you,'* that would be enough."

—Meister Eckhart

TAKE 5

A guaranteed way to grow your assets and see abundance in your life is to acknowledge and be thankful for what you already have. As cliché as it sounds, it's powerful to list all the daily needs that are met in your life—food, clothing, warm bed, public education, etc. Also, think about your relationships, opportunities, and whatever else comes to mind that you enjoy as a part of your daily life.

What are you grateful for today? Write it down in your journal.

Your abundant life

Rest and Refresh

"When the *well's dry*, we know the worth of water."

—Benjamin Franklin

To have energy and stamina to make your life all that it is meant to be, it is important that you are taking care of yourself. Getting rest is one of the most important ways to stay healthy and rejuvenate. It also improves your productivity! Sometimes getting enough sleep can be difficult, especially if you are in a rigorous academic or creative environment. Nonetheless, as often as possible, getting a good night's sleep will improve your well-being.

Also give yourself short five-minute breaks often while working or studying. Taking a few moments to stretch or hydrate with some water will increase your staying-power.

TAKE 5

Right now, take a few minutes to rest and relax. Look through the photos and quotes in this book or simply close your eyes for a few minutes.

Money Matters

Jolie is a smart, creative, and savvy high school student. She loves politics and has invested a tremendous percentage of her high school years understanding community organizing and grassroots movements. Her dream is to be a U.S. diplomat or high-ranking government official. When it came time to attend college, though, Jolie decided to pursue a career in business. She believed it would be easier to find a job, become financially secure, and pay off her student loans. Her hope is to pursue her truest ambitions and reflect who she really is later.

So, she is investing four years of her life in a college education that she is not that interested in, in order to make money and pay for the degree she receives in a subject that she doesn't really care about. A story like this is too common and often continues with a financially lucrative but deeply unfulfilling or a lackluster job, the accumulation of material possessions, and a nagging feeling of emptiness. Does this make any sense to you at all?

Here's the moral of the story. Money does matter, but don't let a short-sighted pursuit of money and the acquisition of material possessions overtake your dreams or stop you from being who you really are. Instead, decide what you really and truly want in life, commit to pursuing it, and then figure out how to simultaneously create the financial abundance you need to make it happen. In the case of Jolie's experience, pursuing her dream of being an international diplomat could have been both a personally and financially fulfilling option.

TAKE 5

For today, think of something that reflects a passion of yours even if it requires some financial investment—like taking a social anthropology course at a science museum, buying a sewing machine to up-cycle clothing, renting a snowboard, etc.

Brainstorm right now some ways you can earn what you need to invest in this passion. Take it a step further, how you might produce income from it.

How Are You Spending Your Assets?

Looking at your checkbook and your schedule is a concrete barometer of how closely your daily life reflects your values and dreams. Maybe you make lots of impulse purchases and so haven't saved as much as you would like. Or there is a particular cause that you feel drawn to, but never volunteered or contributed financially to. Perhaps there is an intriguing architecture course that you have been meaning to save up for or register in, but have never found the time to do it.

> "We can tell our values by looking at our checkbook stubs."[51]
>
> —Gloria Steinem

Have you ever thought about being an entrepreneur?
Take a peek at Chris Guillebeau's book the *$100 Start Up: Reinvent the Way You Make a Living, Do What You Love, and Create a New Future.*

How about making money from your art?
Check out Ann Rea's video interview on the goodlifeproject.com

TAKE 5

Go back and look at Part 4, *Deep-Down Matters*, and think about how you spend your time and money. List three ways that these investments align with your values.

Are there any disconnects between what matters to you deep down and how you spend your time and/or money? If so, write down one straightforward change you could make to invest in something that is more meaningful to you.

Stay in the Driver's Seat

Money is only one tool to *financial freedom*. But don't let it drive you. In other words, don't buy more stuff that you don't need. Maintaining too many possessions will clutter your mind and consume your days. Instead, invest in your personal development and your dreams.

TAKE 5

Write the words: I am investing in my dreams, my financial independence, and me. You might even put it on a card to keep in your wallet.

Next time you want to make an impulse clothing or accessory purchase for immediate gratification, think about your longer term path. Hold off for just two weeks before spending your money on it. Or at minimum, leave the store, take a breath and come back in an hour.

DAY 77

Growing Your Assets Wrap-Up

Money does matter, but also begin to think about growing your assets in a broader way by including your time, your personal development, etc. in your calculation.

Being grateful for what you have is a positive first step in creating abundance in your life. Be sure to take care of yourself to ensure that you are building the reserves of energy and stamina you need to pursue your biggest, boldest dreams.

Your financial health is important and should be a consideration in your plans, but don't lead with the pursuit of material wealth or let it replace your dreams. Think about how you spend your time and money and be sure it matches with what matters to you deep down.

Use the power of affirmations and good old-fashioned delayed gratification to begin to make wise financial decisions.

If there is one BIG takeaway, it is this (we've said it a few times but it bears repeating): you can be financially independent and also live your dreams. You don't have to choose just one or the other—remember that!

TAKE 5

Go back through Days 71–76 and highlight one thing about money and your dreams that surprised you. Be sure to circle or dog-ear what you recorded so you can find it later.

Invest in you!

Quick Review for Days 71–77

- Broaden your definition of assets to include your personal development, time, etc.

- Say "thank you" daily for all the abundance that is already in your life.

- Be sure to rest and rejuvenate to foster the energy you need to pursue your goals.

- Money does matter, but lead with what really matters to you, and then think about how you can make that happen financially.

- Be financially independent and live your dreams! Start by affirming that it's possible and make financial decisions based on your longer-term goals.

grow your assets **REST AND REFRESH** abundance

priceless assets

use money as a tool
foster energy longer-term goals invest DREAMS gratitude
pursue your goals attributes

THE DREAMER'S RITE OF PASSAGE

"To thine own self be true."

—Shakespeare

Using the Power of the Dream Catcher

"You don't need to explain your dreams. They belong to you." [52]

—Paulo Coelho

According to Ojibwe Native American culture, the dream catcher is hung by a sleeping person so that dreams both good and bad pass through before entering the person's mind. As the legend goes, when bad dreams try to crash through, they are caught in the webbing of the dream catcher, causing the nightmare or unimportant dream to melt away and perish. The good dreams, though, flow in via the center of the dream catcher and enter the sleeper's mind. [53]

Just like in the Ojibwe legend, roadblocks may feel like they are attempting to crash in on your desires. You are moving ahead, maybe even giddy with your progress, until there's a stumbling block in your path. Although temporary roadblocks can make even the most focused dreamer question her direction, they don't have to prevent you from seeing your worthiest pursuits through.

Over the next several days, we will be highlighting some typical dream crashers and some ways to stop them from impacting your wildest dreams and everyday musings, letting your good dreams flow through your life center as intended.

Overcoming obstacles is such a universal theme that there are countless songs written about it. Listen to *Stronger* by Kelly Clarkson for just one example.

Innately spectacular you!

Be You-er

> "Today *you are* you! That is **truer** than true!
>
> There is no one alive that is *you-er* than you!"[54]
>
> —Dr. Seuss

It happens to even the most self-assured: comparing yourself to another and coming up short.

No matter the reason, measuring yourself against the perceived status of another person doesn't feel particularly pleasant. The success of others often appears more remarkable from the outside and often the object of your envy may be facing similar struggles (and maybe even comparing themselves to YOU!).

The ginormous problem with comparing yourself to others, though, is that you can lose focus on your own direction and what really matters to you.

TAKE 5

Next time you find yourself comparing yourself to someone else, take a moment and compliment the person (either aloud or in your head) by acknowledging her success. Then think about the reason she is so successful? How can you learn from those to whom you compare yourself?

From there, let your feelings fuel you to continue being even you-er.

Got Support?

"The woman who *follows the crowd* will usually go no further than the crowd. The woman who *walks alone* is likely to find herself in places no one has ever been before."

—attributed to Albert Einstein

TAKE 5

You need support no matter what you are pursuing, but this is particularly true when heading in a direction that is different than that of the crowd. You can never have enough support when going after what you really want. In addition to family and friends, there are a large number of organizations that can help you on your way to reaching for the stars. See the *Resources* in the back of this book if you need a place to get started.

Don't Start with Plan B

What Sarah, a high school student, loves more than anything is cooking. She secretly dreams of going to culinary school. Every chance she gets, she experiments in the kitchen or takes a cooking class. She's been watching the Food Network since she was five years old—but only the serious chefs. She also loves to travel, perform, and just talk—a lot. She secretly wonders what it would be like to travel the world and have her own show on the Food Network.

As she considers her future, she wants to be practical and make a good living (a lot of money, to be honest) so that she can support herself and not have to worry about money. She also wants an important and prestigious job. All noble and sensible, right?

Should Sarah stop considering something as whimsical as pursuing her culinary passions altogether?

There are many options for Sarah. One is to pursue a very practical, secure direction and continue cooking as a hobby. This is sometimes called "Plan B" or a back-up plan. Plan B's sometimes turn out awesome and are good and smart. There is nothing wrong with having a back-up option.

But. . .what if, instead of starting with her back-up plan, Sarah indulged her dreams for even one year and considered what action steps are required to finance and study culinary arts in France? What if she then researched the backgrounds of Food Network chefs (only the serious ones, of course) to determine what their education and experience credentials are? What if she started a food blog or youtube channel tomorrow and shared her recipes online to try this crazy vision on for size? Who knows—could she be the next Nadia G., Giada De Laurentiis, or Rachel Ray?

TAKE 5

Before you settle for Plan B, indulge your most outrageous aspirations for a while. Be sure to write down that dream and then break it down to doable action steps. Plan B will still be there as your back-up.

DAY
82

Go Ahead—Make Mistakes

Babe Ruth is one of the greatest players to play professional baseball. In 1923, he broke the record for the most home runs in a season. Here's the other critical statistic, though: Babe Ruth also struck out more times than any other player in Major League Baseball.

"Every strike brings me closer to the next homerun."[55]

—Babe Ruth

Hate to bring up this pesky point, but just like good old Babe had setbacks, you, too, may face disappointment, failures, and mistakes in your life. That's great news—because it brings you closer to your goal. Even better news, some of the greatest discoveries have occurred thanks to seemingly ridiculous mistakes.

TAKE 5

Learn from your mistakes and setbacks. Keep moving in a positive direction even if you feel afraid or are plagued with self-doubt.

If you hit a roadblock, find a way around it or another path to the same destination, but keep moving forward in the direction of your goals that matter to you deep down.

You've got this!

Make a Choice

Jaime has been an athlete since she fell in love with soccer at her first game at age 5. Now in high school, her original plan was to play both lacrosse and soccer. As it turned out, though, when she received an invitation to an elite, nationally-ranked team, she knew it was time to make a choice—continue to play both sports, which she loved, or give up competitive lacrosse. She decided to go all-in with soccer for one year.

TAKE 5

Some people have one big thing that they are passionate about. Many more have interest in several areas or only vague inclinations, so they feel frozen with indecision. The fear often is picking the wrong thing.

Take your time by investigating and exploring several options that interest you. That's productive and smart, but at some point you have to make a choice. Remember, not choosing is, in fact, choosing something.

DAY 84

The Dreamer's Rite of Passage Wrap-up

Like every dreamer, you will likely come across stumbling blocks as you head in a positive direction toward your mightiest dreams. Rather than let these obstacles derail your quests, learn from them and continue to move forward. Dream crashers can take many forms, from comparing yourself to others to starting with Plan B before you have indulged in your most exciting dreams. Everyone makes mistakes. In fact, some of the greatest discoveries have occurred thanks to seemingly ridiculous mistakes. Play, explore, research, but then choose, because not choosing is in fact making a big choice! You'll need support on your travels, so make sure you reach out and find it!

Check out J.K. Rowling author of the *Harry Potter* series, for just one inspiring example of overcoming obstacles to reach a dream.

TAKE 5

Go back through Days 78–83 and highlight one aha moment you had. Be sure to circle or dog-ear what you recorded so you can find it later.

Quick Review for Days 78–84

- ❤ Obstacles or dream crashers may come your way, but don't let them prevent you from heading in a positive direction.
- ❤ Be you-er rather than comparing yourself to another.
- ❤ Everyone needs support, especially when heading in a direction that's new or different from the crowd.
- ❤ Don't start with Plan B.
- ❤ Go ahead and make mistakes.
- ❤ When it's time, make a choice.

positive direction choosing

what's your plan A?

DREAM CATCHER

investigating *BE YOU-ER*

make mistakes GOALS

explore SUPPORT move forward

TAKE 5 FOR YOUR DREAMS

CONCLUSION

WHAT'S YOUR BRAVE?

ASTOUND YOUR WORLD

"Go confidently in the direction of your dreams.
Live the life you have imagined."

—Henry David Thoreau

Take-5-Aways

Well, that's just about a wrap. . . almost. Let what has impacted you the most stay with you on your journey long after your Take 5's are complete. Beginning today, review each section and record what you dog-eared or circled in your journal. Or something that you did that surprised you, maybe a discovery you made about yourself. You decide! What are your big take-aways?

DAY 85

A Place for Daily Goodness

Take-away: _____

_____

_____

DAY 86

Being Who You Really Are

Take-away: _____

_____

_____

ONE in 7 billion

DAY **87**

Be YOU-er!

What's Love Got to Do with It?

Take-away: _____

_____

_____

DAY **88**

Deep-Down Matters

Take-away: _____

_____

_____

DAY **89**

Seeing Your Future

Take-away: _____

_____

_____

DAY **90**

How Your Dreams Come True

Take-away: _____

_____

_____

DAY **91**

Be Brave

Take-away: _____

_____

_____

DAY **92**

Your Passion Tribe

Take-away: _____

_____

_____

DAY **93**

The Secret to Developing Your Superpowers

Take-away: _____

_____

_____

Love what you do

DAY **94**

Body Brave

Take-away: _____

_____

_____

DAY **95**

Growing Your Assets

Take-away: _____

_____

_____

DAY **96**

Dreamer's Rite of Passage

Take-away: _____

_____

_____

You matter!

> "The future belongs to those who
> believe in the *beauty of their dreams.*"
>
> — attributed to Eleanor Roosevelt

Well in closing, may we say... Wow! Yippee! You did it! You are astounding!

You have completed over 100 pages of daily goodness and are on the path to making your one-of-a-kind, never-to-be-on-this-planet-again life all that it was meant to be. We can see the glow from here—that radiance on a woman's face when she explains with confidence how she is creating a life of passion and purpose! And now that someone is you!

Even though this is the end of the book, keep going to your daily place of goodness and taking action every day to nurture the superstar that you are! And above all else,

keep being you!

TAKE 5

And the Final Take 5 is....

Sign up for regular goodies of inspiration and support as you continue on your path at take5foryourdreams.com!

Let us know how you are doing, OK? Share your stories, your aha moments, your stumbling blocks, your questions.... Your story will inspire someone else too!

A sampling of additional encouragement and inspiration for you as you Take 5 for Your Dreams.

What's Your Brave?
website + ebooks

Join us at:
www.take5foryourdreams.com
www.whatsyourbrave.com

Free e-books when you sign up:
- ♥ *Body Brave*
- ♥ *Getting it RigHt the First Time*

Role Models

Bethelem Tilahun Alemu, Founder of soleRebels (solerebelsfootwear.co)

Molly Barker, Girls On The Run (girlsontherun.org)

Sara Blakely, Founder of Spanx (spanx.com)

Julia Bluhm, Teen Activist, (sparksummit.com)

Ursula Burns, CEO of Xerox

Lena Dunham,
Actor and Creator of *Girls*

Caterina Fake, Co-Founder of flickr and hunch (hunch.com)

Bethany Hamilton, Surfer (bethanyhamilton.com)

Kamala Harris,

California Attorney General

Sejal Hathi, Co-Founder of girltank (girltank.org)

Dani Johnson, Entrepreneur (danijohnson.com)

Maya Lin, Architect

Gabriella Runnels, Founder of it onlytakesagirl.org (itonlytakesagirl.org)

Deb Sterling, Goldie Blox™ (goldieblox.com, http://www. upworthy.com/move-over-barbie-8212-youre-obsolete?g=2)

Additional Sources for Role Model Videos, Articles, and more

Forbes, Women to Watch (forbes.com)

Makers (makers.com)

TEDx (ted.com)

Organizations to Inspire and Make a Difference

BUILD (build.org)

Campaign for a Commercial-Free Childhood (commercialfreechildhood.org)

Change.org (change.org)

Charity: Water (charitywater.org)

Cradles to Crayons (cradlestocrayons.org)

Do Something (dosomething.org)

Girls On The Run (girlsontherun.org)

Girltank (girltank.org)

Girl UP (GirlUp.org)

LitWorld (litworld.org)

Miss Representation (missrepresentation.org)

One Billion Rising (onebillionrising.org)

Pencils of Promise (pencilsofpromise.org)

Spark Summit (sparksummit.com)

The Girl Effect (girleffect.org)

Books, Media, and Websites for Education, Motivation, and Encouragement

am I being kind (thekindnesscenter.com)

Art of Non-Conformity (chrisguillebeau.com)

Leo Babuta (zenhabits.net)

Joshua Becker (becomingminimalist.com)

Brené Brown (brenebrown.com)

Kris Carr (Kriscarr.com)

Jonathan Fields (goodlifeproject.com)

Marie Forleo (marieforleo.com)

Hardy Girls Healthy Women (hghw.org)

I Am That Girl (iamthatgirl.com)

Danielle LaPorte (daniellelaporte.com)

Miss Representation (missrepresentation.org)

Suze Orman (suzeorman.com)

Packaging Girlhood (packaginggirlhood.com)

Gretchen Rubin (happiness-project.com)

Kyle Rutkin (kylerutkin.com)

Science Club for Girls (scienceclubforgirls.org)

Smart Girls at the Party (smartgirlsattheparty.com)

SPARK Summit (sparksummit.com)

Think (lisabloom.com)

Tinybuddha.com

Oprah Winfrey (www.oprah.com/own)

Wishcraft (barbarasher.com)

zenpencils.com

Organizations to Expand Your Passion Tribe

Artists for Humanity (afhboston.org)

Girls for a Change (girlsforachange.org)

Girls Inc. (girlsinc.org)

Girls LEAP (leapmail.wix.com/girlsleap)

Girls On The Run (girlsontherun.org)

Girl Up (girlup.org)

Science Club for Girls (scienceclubforgirls.org)

Additional resources can be found at www.whatsyourbrave.com

[1] Oliver, Mary, *New and Selected Poems, A Summer Day*, Beacon Press, 1992.

[2] DePaola, John, original source unknown.

[3] Babauta, Leo, Zen Habits, www.zenhabits.net, (Last accessed: February 2013)

[4] Rodgers and Hammerstein, *My Own Little Corner*, 1957.

[5] Dachis, Adam, *How Muscle Memory Works and How it Affects Your Success*, http://lifehacker.com/5799234/how-muscle-memory-works-and-how-it-affects-your-success (Last accessed: February 2013)

[6] Original heard during a bat mitzvah service by one awesome rabbi.

[7] Merriam-Webster Dictionary, http://www.merriam-webster.com/dictionary/genius (Last accessed: February 2013)

[8] cummings, e. e., original source unknown.

[9] Startwithwhy.com (Last accessed: September 2012)

[10] Young, Margaret, original source unknown.

[11] Thurman, Howard, original source unknow.

[12] Sher, Barbara, *Wishcraft*.

[13] Guillebeau, Chris, *Art of Non-Conformity: Set Your Own Rules, Live the Life You Want, and Change the World*, Perigee, 2010, www.chrisguillebeau.com.

[14] Baumeister, Vohs, Aaker, Garbinsky, *Some Key Differences Between a Happy and Meaningful Life*, http://faculty-gsb.stanford.edu/aaker/pages/documents/SomeKeyDifferencesHappyLifeMeaningfulLife_2012.pdf (Last accessed: February 2013)

[15] www.kickstarter.com

[16] *Goldi Blox™* kickstarter video, *Upworthy*, http://www.upworthy.com/move-over-barbie-8212-youre-obsolete?g=2 (Last accessed: February 2013)

[17] Frank, Anne, original source unknown.

[18] *What's Your Brave is a writing and media project for parents and teen girls committed to giving young women the knowledge and resources they need to live their one beautiful life bravely. To find out more, go to:* www.whatsyourbrave.com

[19] *What's Your Brave*, www.whatsyourbrave.com

[20] Einstein, Albert, original source unknown.

[21] Starr, Pamela Vaull, original source unknown.

[22] Steinem, Gloria, www.gloriasteinem.com, (Last accessed: March 2013)

[23] *The Life and Legacy of Rachel Carson*, www.rachelcarson.org (Last accessed: February 2013)

[24] Gandhi, Mahatma, original source unknown.

[25] Curie, Marie, original source unknown.

[26] Forleo, Marie, www.marieforleo.com, (Last accessed: March 2013)

[27] Nasol, Katherine, *What's Your Brave*, www.whatsyourbrave.com

[28] Anonymous, *What's Your Brave*, www.whatsyourbrave.com

[29] Carson, Rachel, *The Sense of Wonder*, New York Harper and Row, 1965.

[30] Winfrey, Oprah, original source unknown.

[31] Brown, Brené, *Daring Greatly: How the Courage to Be Vulnerable Transforms the Way We Live, Love, Parent, and Lead*, Gotham, 2012, www.brenebrown.com.

[32] *Why Sharing Secrets is Good for Teens' Health*, *Wall Street Journal* online, February 4, 2013.

[33] Earhart, Amelia, original source unknown.

[34] Colvin, Geoffrey, *What It Takes to Be Great*, *CNN Money online*, originally printed in *Fortune Magazine*, October 2006.

[35] CNN interview with Coretta Scott King, 2003, www.cnn.com.

[36] Biography.com, *Pink Biography*, www.biography.com/people/pink (Last accessed: February 2013)

[37]Startwithwhy.com (Last accessed: September 2012)

[38]*What's Your Brave*, www.whatsyourbrave.com

[39]Babauta, Leo, Zen Habits, www.zenhabits.net, (Last accessed: February 2013)

[40]Carr, Kris, *Crazy Sexy Diet: Eat Your Veggies, Ignite Your Spark, and Live Like You Mean It*, skirt!, Globe Pequot Press, 2011, www.kriscarr.com.

[41]Women's Sports Foundation, *The Women's Sports Foundation Report*, www.womensportsfoundation.org, (Last accessed: May 2012)

[42]American Psychological Association, *Report of the Task Force on the Sexualization of Girls*, http://www.apa.org/pi/women/programs/girls/report.aspx (Last accessed: September 2012)

[43]American Psychological Association, *Report of the Task Force of the Sexualization of Girls.*

[44]Created by: Jean Kilbourne, Directed by: Sut Jhally, *Killing Me Softly* documentary, www. mediaed.org (Last accessed: May 2012)

[45]Grieco, Paula, *Body Brave*, www.whatsyourbrave.com (Last accessed February 2013)

[46]Go to www.missrepresentation.org and considering watching their documentary for more information.

[47]*What's Your Brave*, www.whatsyourbrave.com

[48]*What's Your Brave*, www.whatsyourbrave.com

[49]Chobsky, Stephen, as heard on NPR interview on *The Perks of Being a Wallflower.*

[50]Ensler, Eve, *The Vagina Monologues*, Random House, www.vday.org.

[51]Steinem, Gloria, original source unknown.

[52]Coelho, Paulo, original source unknown.

[53]*Dream Catchers*, www.dream-catchers.org (Last accessed: February 2013)

[54]Dr. Seuss, *Happy Birthday to You!*, Random House, 1959.

[55]Ruth, Babe, www.baberuth.com.